DOWN TO THE LETTER

Daily Devotional and Prayer Guide

Dorie Sammons

CONTENTS

INTRODUCTION

"Down to the Letter" means Attention to detail. The goal of this book is to remind us that God is in every detail of our lives.

"Lord, we ask that you guide us through the next two months. Open our eyes to the glory of Your word. Bring us wisdom and grace through these verses and stories, as we lift praises to Your name. Amen."

ANGER

Anger is a strong, negative emotion, one that is hard to reverse. When we get angry, our heart races, our blood pressure rises, and for many, we can feel physically sick. All of this is almost instant. Calming down these feelings takes much longer and starts with several deep breaths.

James 1:19-20, My dear brothers, take note of this: Everyone should be quick to listen, slow to speak, and slow to become angry. For man's anger does not bring about the righteous life that God desires.

Ephesians 4:26b-27, Do not let the sun go down while you are still angry, and do not give the devil a foothold.

If we let anger take hold, it leaves an open door for Satan to walk right in, and revenge can consume us. Remember sisters, it is God's job to judge, not ours.

Matthew 7:1, "Do not judge, or you too will be judged."

Instead, pray! Pray out loud, shout if you have to. God's Grace can calm your soul and bring you peace. His love will slow your heart, so you can begin to breathe normally again. Anger is not an attribute we want to let fester. Satan thrives on these kinds of feelings and would love for you to leave the door cracked so he can keep jabbing and prodding until you hit a breaking point. We are not going to let that happen. Again, deep breaths and PRAY!

"Lord Jesus, take me by the hand, bring me to my knees in your presence. I pray that you will take away the negative emotions and fill me with love and joy. Bring me a peace that only you can. Amen."

Prayer prompts:
Pray for God to free you of all anger.
Pray for a friend or neighbor who is facing trials.
Pray that your family can wake each morning knowing God's grace is with them.
Pray for God's calming peace.

Notes:

Use this page to write out your prayer...

ATTITUDE

"Whether you think you can or think you can't, you're right." I saw this on a t-shirt at a sporting event recently, and how true! We decide each morning how we want to start our day. Cranky because the weather is gray and rainy, or happy because God has blessed us with a fresh, renewing rain. Our attitude is all in our perception of what is going on around us.

Romans 15:5 "May the God who gives endurance and encouragement give you the same attitude of mind toward each other that Christ Jesus had." Philippians 2:5, "Your attitude should be the same as that of Christ Jesus".

One of my favorite authors, Patsy Clairmont, said in her book Sportin' a 'Tude, "Stinky attitudes are airborne. They waft around and add to the pollution on planet earth." Nobody wants to be around that. Attitude is a choice. You can choose to be like Christ or choose to pollute those around you. What choice will you make?

Hebrews 4:12, For the word of God is alive and active. Sharper than any double-edged sword, it penetrates even to dividing soul and spirit, joints and marrow; it judges the thoughts and attitudes of the heart.

God is watching. He knows when our attitude is not that of Christ Jesus. When you stand before the pearly gates, will you be able to look Him in the face?

"Lord Jesus, hear my prayer. I kneel before you humbled, wanting to be like you. Grant me wisdom and peace to make the right decisions in life, to choose the right attitude in every situation... Amen"

Prayer Prompts:
Do you start your day with a positive attitude? Or do you let things bring you down before you've even had your morning coffee? Pray for God to help you start your day on the right track. To give you the tools to choose a more positive approach.

Notes:

Use this page to write out your prayer...

BELIEVE

John 3:16, "For God so loved the world, that he gave His only Son, that whoever believes in Him, will not parish, but have eternal life."

This verse is always the first that comes to mind when we talk about God's love for us. His love is so amazing. He loves us so much, that he sacrificed Jesus, His Son.

John 6:35, "I am the bread of life. He who comes to me will never go hungry. And he who believes in me will never be thirsty." And 40, "For my Fathers will is that everyone who looks to the Son and believes in Him shall have eternal life, and I will raise him up at the last day."

To believe in something you cannot see is taking a leap of faith.

Hebrews 11:6, "And without faith it is impossible to please God, because anyone who comes to Him must believe that He exists and that He rewards those who earnestly seek Him."

Our entire faith revolves around the belief that a glorious God created us from dust. His son was born of a Virgin, and then died to forgive our sins. Then Jesus rose from the grave to ascend and prepare us a place. Some might look at this and say we're crazy, but we know better.

We know that God is gracious and merciful. He loves us beyond measure. And he looks over us, guides and protects us from evil. He sent Jesus to heal the sick and work miracles as He preached to crowds of people to share our father's love. Jesus is our proof. The Bible is our truth!

"Thank you, Father God, for loving us the way you do. We praise you for all you have done for us and for giving us your son to show us the way to our home in heaven. Thank you, Jesus, for dying on that cross, for your body and blood that were shed for us. Praise you Jesus.   Amen."

Prayer Prompts:
Pray for the unbelievers, that they will be open to learning of God's love.
Pray for your neighbors, friends, family members.
Pray for God to show you how you can share God's love.

Notes:

Use this page to write out your prayer...

BE STILL

Life, that thing that keeps us running in multiple directions at all times. We are so busy doing "Life", that we sometimes forget to enjoy it. How often are we struggling because we are juggling too many things? Take a breath! God is here to help us through. He is our guide and will lead us and fight for us. There is no need to struggle, just STOP!

Exodus 14:14, The Lord will fight for you, you need only to be still."

What does that mean, be still? It means just that. Stop and listen. You can't hear God through all the noise and bustle.

Psalm 46:10, He says," Be still and know that I am God; I will be exalted among the nations, I will be exalted in the earth."

Take a moment to be with God, truly with Him. Close your eyes, listen to the birds' chirp, the wind blow, and know that God is right there beside you.

1 Kings 19:11b-12, Then a great and powerful wind tore the mountains apart and shattered the rocks before the Lord, but the Lord was not in the wind. After the wind there was an earthquake, but the Lord was not in the earthquake. After the earthquake came a fire, but the Lord was not in the fire. After the fire came a gentle whisper.

Be still and listen. God's voice may be but a whisper. Be still so that you do not miss what he needs to tell you.

"Lord, I am listening. In the wind, in the breeze, I am listening. I hear your voice in the melody of the birds in the trees. In the silence Lord, I am listening. Amen"

Prayer Prompts:
Praise God for all he has done in your life. Ask him to speak to you, and then just "be still" and listen. You may not get a verbal response, but you never know what you might hear if you just listen.

Notes:

Use this page to write out your prayer...

CHOICES

Genesis 1:1, In the beginning God created the Heavens and the earth.

Genesis 2:7, the Lord God formed the man from the dust of the ground and breathed into his nostrils the breath of life, and the man became a living being. In verse 18, God decided man should not be alone, and in verse 27, He creates woman. You all know the rest of the story. Today's lesson is more about humanity as a whole, a few hundred or so years later.

Psalm 100:3, Know that the Lord is God. It is he who made us, and we are his; we are his people, the sheep of his pasture.

1 Chronicles 16:13, you his servants the descendants of Israel, his chosen ones, the children of Jacob.

All humanity was created by God, but not all choose to follow Jesus in righteousness. God has given each of us free will. The ability to make our own choices. And with that, He also gave us the knowledge to know right from wrong. Those who choose to follow Jesus will get to live an eternity in Heaven with Jesus at God's right hand.

John 14:2, My Father's house has many rooms, if that were not so, would I have told you that I am going there to prepare a place for you? So, God chose to create us so that we could choose to follow Jesus. And because we choose Jesus, we have a home in heaven.

"Our Father who art in heaven, we are so thankful that you sent your son Jesus. We praise your name and exalt you on high. You gave us life and free will, yet we want to follow, we want to live a righteous life in the presence of your glory. We choose to be your children. Amen."

Prayer Prompts:
Pray for your own children, grandchildren
Pray for a neighbor or friend who does not know Jesus
Praise God for creating us and giving us a home in heaven.

Notes:

Use this page to write out your prayer...

COMMUNICATION

Ephesians 4:29, Let no corrupt communication proceed out of your mouth, but that which is good to the use of edifying, that it may minister grace unto the hearers.

Ok, I admit I had to use the King James version to get the word "communication". The newer versions say *"Don't use foul or abusive language. Let everything you say be good and helpful, so that your words will be an encouragement to those who hear them."*

Your momma was right. If you can't say something nice, don't say anything at all. How we communicate with others says a lot about the person we are. Can others see God in you? In your words, your actions? Maybe the 11th commandment should have been…do not curse. I know a lot of people that would have trouble with that one.

Hebrews 13:16, (KJV)But to do good and to communicate forget not: for with such sacrifices God is well pleased. (NIV)And don't forget to do good and to share with those in need. These are the sacrifices that please God.

Good works will not get you to Heaven, but they are expected in order to show God that we honor Him. This reminds me of the parable of the

Good Samaritan found in Luke 10:25-37. Three people came across this man on the road, the least likely person was the one to show kindness. To communicate God's love through his actions.

"Lord, help me to be more like the Samaritan. To show grace and kindness in my actions. Help me to have the heart of Jesus. Amen."

Prayer prompts:
Is there someone you know that needs to know Jesus? Do you witness to them through your actions? Ask God to show you how to be more like Jesus. To help you to help others. Pray for ways you can help in your neighborhood or community, or even your child's school.

Notes:

Use this page to write out your prayer…

COMPASSION

Psalm 116:5, The lord is gracious and righteous; our God is full of compassion. There are so many times in the Bible where God has shown compassion for his people. Jesus dying on the cross is one of the biggest examples. All to save us from our sinful nature.

How about Jonah? God told him to go to Nineveh because they were overwrought with sin. Afraid, Jonah went the other direction, running and trying to hide from God. Well, that did not work out well. Jonah ended up on a boat and God sent a storm to "rock the boat", so to speak.

Jonah told the crew to throw him from the boat to save themselves, so they did. Instead of letting Jonah die, God showed compassion and sent a whale to give him a ride to guess where… Nineveh. Jonah told the people God's message, that Nineveh would be overturned in 40 days. *Jonah 3:10, When God saw what they did and how they turned from their evil ways, he had compassion it did not bring upon them the destruction he had threatened.*

God shows us compassion and in return Expects us to do the same. *Colossians 3:12, Therefore, as God's chosen people, holy and dearly loved, clothe yourselves with compassion, kindness, humil-*

ity, gentleness, and patience.

"Lord, help me to show compassion to those around me. To lead by example as you have taught me to do. Thank you, Lord, for showing me your love and compassion, as I have not always felt deserving. Praise you, in Jesus name. Amen."

Prayer Prompts:
Pray through Psalm 51:1
Have mercy on me, oh God, according to your unfailing love; according to your great compassion blot out all my transgressions.

Notes:

Use this page to write out your prayer...

DAZED AND CONFUSED

Have you ever woken up feeling lethargic, your eyes don't want to open, and your limbs feel heavy? You just want to go back to sleep! How about a situation where something happens so quickly, that you aren't sure what just happened? Here's one, you walk into class expecting a study hall, and the teacher says to pull out a pencil and paper for a pop quiz. What?!

Can you picture the dazed look on Jonah's face just as he realized a whale was going to EAT him? Or the confusion when the disciples started passing around 5 loaves of bread and two fish for 5000 people? No matter the situation, or how dazed and confused we may be, God has got this! He is always working, even behind the scenes when we least expect it.

John 5:17, "but Jesus answered them, my father has been working until now, he has never ceased working, and I too am working."

We can always rely on our Heavenly Father to guide us toward the path He has chosen for us... *John 13:7, "Jesus replied, you do not realize now what I am doing, but later you will understand."* When you hear that little voice in the back of your head, you should probably listen. It may be telling you what your next move is along the path. We never know who or what God will send to help us on our way.

"Lord, give me clarity to listen to your voice, and wisdom to follow where you lead. I want to be your servant Lord. To go where you need me and do what you command. Help me to see clearly all those you place before me. To know they are here to help and guide me on your behalf. Amen."

Prayer Prompts:
As God is working in your life, ask how you can help others.
Pray for ways to help in your community.
Pray for guidance.

Notes:

Use this page to write out your prayer...

DOUBT

A feeling of uncertainty or lack of conviction. Fear of the unknown. In the book of John, we find Thomas doubting the resurrection of Christ. He must see Jesus to believe he is really alive.

John 20:27, Then He said to Thomas, "put your finger here; see my hands. Reach out your hand and put it into my side. Stop doubting and believe." 2 Corinthians 5:7, *"We live by faith, not by sight."*

Doubt and Faith cannot co-exist. For Thomas, his doubt overshadowed his faith in Jesus. He had to see to believe. And what about Peter in Matthew 14:22-33. Peter jumped out of the boat and started walking toward Jesus. He did not start to sink until he started to doubt.

We all have doubts and fears in our lives. That is when we most need to turn to our Faith and let Jesus take the wheel, (as Carrie Underwood would say). *Jude 1:22, Be merciful to those who doubt.* Look to the Heavens and know that God is with you. He's got this!

"Father in Heaven help to keep my Faith strong and give me wisdom to overcome my

doubts. Guide me Lord to make the right choices
every day. Amen."

Prayer Prompts:
Help in our daily walk with God
Guidance and wisdom in making decisions
Faith to overcome doubt and fear

Notes:

Use this page to write out your prayer...

DRAGON

Because every great book has a dragon... *Revelation 12:9, The great dragon was hurled down – that ancient serpent called the devil, or Satan, who leads the whole world astray. He was hurled to the earth and his angels with him.*

Unfortunately, this dragon is not a good one. He is the evil of all evils, Satan himself. Notice, the dragon in Revelations is the same serpent that spoke to Eve in Genesis. He is part of Bible history from beginning to end, just like God, our Alpha and Omega. A book would not be good without conflict. You always have good versus evil to keep the plot going. It is scary though when you realize this is no piece of fiction. This is a non-fiction documentary. And evil is fighting us every step of the way.

Romans 12:21, *Do not be overcome by evil, but overcome evil with good.*

Ephesians 6:11, Put on the full armor of God, so that you can take your stand against the devil's schemes.

Pray daily, every hour if necessary, to keep evil at bay. Ask God to protect you and guide you in the light. Think about it, what if you were Eve? What do you think you would have done? Me, well

I'm not a big fan of apples, but I wouldn't have known that until after that first bite. I'd like to think I would have said no and walked away, but chances are that every one of us would have fallen for the hype and ate the fruit.

Good news is, that because Eve took that bite, we all now know right from wrong. We all have free will and can make our own choices. We now have to decide for ourselves what to do next. So, PRAY EVERYDAY! Ask for guidance from the one true light.

"Jesus, you are the way, the truth, and the light. Lead us out of darkness and into the light. Guide us toward your truth and lead the way to Heaven where our Father awaits us. Amen."

Prayer Prompts:
Ask for God's wisdom to make right choices in life
Protection from evil of all kinds
Guidance to follow the path he has chosen for us
Footprints to follow the light.

Notes:

Use this page to write out your prayer...

ENCOURAGE

Encouragement is something that everyone needs. There are several places in the Bible that back that up. *2 Thessalonians 2:17, Encourage your hearts and strengthen you in every good deed and word. Romans 15:4, For everything that was written in the past was written to teach us, so that through the endurance taught in the scriptures and the encouragement they provide, we might hope.*

Our church family is our greatest source of encouragement. Our pastors, small group leaders, our friends are all there to help us in times of need and encourage us to stand strong. In return we are to encourage others. Help our neighbors, co-workers, even a stranger on the street. Teach them that our God is good!

2 Timothy 4:2, Preach the word; be prepared in season and out of season; correct, rebuke, and encourage – with great patience and careful instruction.

We are all Christ's disciples. We have all been tasked with preaching God's word and teaching others about our Lord and Savior.

Romans 12:8, if it is to encourage, then give encouragement; if it is giving, then give generously, if it is to lead, do it diligently, if it is to show mercy, do it cheerfully.

"Lord, show me your will for me. Help me to know how to teach your word to others and to encourage them. Shine your blessings on all who seek you. Amen."

Prayer Prompts:
Pray for encouragement
Pray for knowledge to encourage others
Pray for the words to preach God's grace
Pray blessings on all God's people

Notes:

Use this page to write out your prayer…

ENVY

A feeling of discontented or resentful longing for someone else's possessions, qualities, or luck; jealousy. *Proverbs 14:30, A heart at peace gives life to the body, but envy rots the bones.* Envy, or jealousy, brings us to Genesis chapter 4. Here we find Cain and Abel. God found favor with Abel's offering of his finest calf, but rebuked Cain's offering from his field. Cain was so jealous of his brother that he murdered him. I would like to point out here that this is not a recommended form of settling difference with your siblings.

Luke 15:11-32 gives us the parable of the prodigal son. The father gives his youngest son half his money, and the boy heads out to squander it away. Meanwhile, the older brother stays home and helps his father run the farm. When the younger son returns home broke and hungry, he is welcomed with open arms. The older brother feels envy and doesn't understand his father's behavior. This father, not unlike our Heavenly Father, welcomed home his lost child.

1 Peter 2:11, Therefore, rid yourself of all malice and all deceit, hypocrisy, envy, and slander of every kind. God just wants what is best for us. He even left 99 sheep in a pen while he went back for one.

"Father take away all envious thoughts. Open are minds and hearts to your Glory. Give us a sense of peace and contentment. Amen."

Prayer Prompts:
Pray that God will keep all envious thoughts from our minds.
Praise Him, pray through your favorite worship song.

Notes:

Use this page to write out your prayer...

FEAR

Psalm 23:4, "Even though I walk through the Valley of the shadow of death, I will fear no evil, you are with me; your rod and your staff, they comfort me." Most of us have read or even memorized the 23rd Psalm. It tells us that God is always with us, therefore we have nothing to fear. Still, we have fears. Things that worry us and keep us awake at night.

Make a list of what you fear most in life. When you look over that list, it probably has things that we fear for our children, or fears about our job, or our bills. Maybe the first thing on your list is spiders. *Psalm 56:3-4, "When I am afraid, I put my trust in you. In God, whose word I praise, in God I trust; I shall not be afraid. What can flesh do to me?"* OK, spiders aren't flesh, so for them get a shoe or some bug spray. I should probably tell you to not kill one of God's creatures, but I'm just keeping it real. Now, for everything else, PRAY! Give it all to God.

Psalm 27:1, "The Lord is my light and my Salvation; whom shall I fear? The Lord is the stronghold of my life; of whom shall I be afraid?" Giving all your fears to God in prayer will give you a piece that only He can give. *Luke 14:27, "Peace I leave with you; my peace I give to you. Not as the world gives do I give to you. Let not your hearts be troubled, neither let them be afraid."* Accept the peace He offers and praise Him. God will always have your back. All you need to do is ask and PRAY!

"Father, I just ask that you guide me through the valley. Take away my fear and replace it with peace. Help me to maintain a calm in my life. Help me to overcome all that frightens me…Amen."

Prayer Prompts:
Now this is where you make that list of fears.
Write it all out and then give it to God.
Use your list to continue the prayer above.

Notes:

Use this page to write out your prayer...

FELLOWSHIP

There are many times in the Bible where Jesus is preaching on a mountainside to thousands of people. We are meant to gather in His name, to have fellowship with other believers. To rely on each other and build each other up.

Matthew 18:20, "For where two or more gather in my name, there I am with them." Acts 2:42, "They devoted themselves to the apostles' teaching and to fellowship, to the breaking of bread, and to prayer."

Our church family is our "village". The phrase "it takes a village" is so very true. No-one can do everything alone. We all need our "family" to hold us up, and we are there for them as well. Most churches also have small groups, or life groups. These are your more immediate family members. The people you do everyday life with, pray with, and study God's Word with.

1John 1:7, "But if we walk in the light, we have fellowship with one another, and the blood of Jesus, his Son, purifies us from all sin." Proverbs 27:17, "As iron sharpens iron, so one man sharpens another."

It is important as a Christian, that we surround ourselves with other Christians.

1 Corinthians 15:33, "Do not be misled: bad

company corrupts good character." This shows us how important it is to "do life" with the right people. So, today reach out to your "sisters". Pray together, and for each other.

"Lord, I lift up my sisters in Christ, my small group members and my church. Bless them Lord, and comfort them, give them peace. Amen"

Prayer Prompts:
Pastors
Small Group leaders
Church Deacons and Elders
Your "Village"

Use this page to write out your prayer...

FORGIVENESS

Luke 17:3-4, "If your brother or sister sins against you, rebuke them; and if they repent, forgive them. Even if they sin against you seven times in a day and seven times come back to you saying, 'I repent,' you must forgive them."

Forgiveness is a powerful thing. It is commanded by God that we forgive those who sin against us, just as God forgives our sins. He sacrificed His only son to wash away our sins and open up a place in Heaven for us.

John 3:16, For God so loved the world that He gave His one and only Son, that whoever believes in him shall not perish but have eternal life. Romans 5:8, But God demonstrates his own love for us in this: While we were still sinners, Christ died for us.

Now, I know this is not as easy as it sounds. Not all sins are created equal... if someone breaks your favorite toy, i.e. cell phone, iPad, hover board...(insert here), we can eventually replace it and forgive them. Grandma's antique punch bowl might take a little longer. If they hurt your feelings, or cause personal injury, that too is harder, but you still MUST forgive them. *Colossians 3:13, Bear with each other and forgive one another if any of you has a grievance against someone. Forgive as the*

Lord forgave you.

"Lord, I really need help on this one. Help me to forgive those who have sinned against me. Give me a sense of peace and understanding toward them... Amen."

Prayer Prompts:
This is another very personal topic. Some of us have some big issues to deal with that make for-giving a very hard thing to do. Is there someone you have been holding a grudge against for a long time? Someone who has hurt you in any way, that you just can't seem to get past. Try writing them a letter (that you will later burn, not mail) that says exactly how you feel. How and why they hurt you. Pray that God will help you to process your thoughts and bring you a peace. Then you will be able to let go of the pain and finally forgive. I am not saying this is going to be easy, but you have to make peace with yourself in order to make peace with God.

Notes:

Use this page to write out your prayer...

GARDENING

What better place to start this one, than Genesis? God created the Heavens and the earth, then created man to inhabit the earth. *Genesis 2:8, "Now the Lord God had planted a garden in the east, in Eden, and there He put the man He had formed."*

We were meant to be gardeners. To take care of the wonderful garden God created for us. Me, I love gardening, but I do not have a green thumb. My tomatoes survive only by the grace of God.

As we move on, another example of gardening in the Bible is found in John 15:1-17. These are the passages of the vine and the branches. *John 15:5, I am the vine; you are the branches. If a man remains in me, and I in him, he will bear much fruit.*

Jesus is the true vine, and God is the gardener. Gardens do not thrive on their own, they need tending. *Isaiah 18:5, For before the harvest, when the blossom is gone and the flower becomes a ripening grape, he will cut off the shoots with pruning knives, and cut down and take away the spreading branches.*

Now, let's say we are the garden. We need to feed the garden by reading the Bible. Study the Word in depth. Pick a book of the Bible and dig into scripture.

2 Timothy 3:16, All Scripture is breathed out by God and profitable for teaching, for reproof, for correction, and for training in righteousness.

"Father God, we ask that you teach us in your word and train us up to be leaders to spread your word to others. Guide us through the pages to tend our Gardens through scripture. Amen"

Prayer Prompts:
Pray for God to give you the verses He wants you to learn from. To guide you through the Bible for a more in-depth relationship with Him.

Notes:

Use this page to write out your prayer...

GRACE

Have you seen the movie "Footloose"? The original where John Lithgow plays the minister? I can picture the scene where he is rehearsing a passionate "Fire and Brimstone" sermon.

But the bible doesn't JUST teach of hell fire and demons, an eye for an eye. It promises a loving God who shows mercy and gives grace.

Ephesians 2:8, For it is by grace you have been saved, through faith – and this is not from yourselves, it is a gift of God. Jesus Himself is our saving grace. In John 3:16, we are told how God sent His son, Jesus, to die for our forgiveness and graced us with the promise of Heaven.

Titus 2:11, For the grace of God has appeared that offers salvation to all people. 2 Timothy 2:1, You then my son, be strong in the grace that is in Christ Jesus.

"Lord, you are a compassionate and gracious

God. Show me your grace, that I may be gracious to others... Amen."

Prayer Prompts:
Pray for how to embrace Grace in everyday life.
Ask for God's grace to empower you.

Notes:

Use this page to write out your prayer...

GRADUATION

The year 2020 will go down in the history books, and not in a good way. In March, the world stopped spinning. That is to say, that life as we know it changed significantly. Schools closed short an entire quarter, businesses closed their doors, and anyone who could, worked from home. All this because a pandemic swept across the planet.

Seniors missed out on Proms and Graduation Ceremonies. All grades missed saying goodbye to friends, and that last day celebration with their teachers. Fall isn't looking much better. Many schools are still closed and are starting the year online at home.

To graduate, simply means to complete something. In this case, they all get to graduate to the next level, it just feels weird without the proper sendoff.

Jesus didn't get a very good sendoff either. He died nailed to a cross, jeered, and rejected by many. Why? Because they feared Him. Luckily for us, this is not where the story ends. On the third day, He rose from the grave, and in that moment our sins were forgiven, and we were all given a clean slate.

1 Peter 1:3. "Praise be to the God and Father of our Lord Jesus Christ! In His great mercy He has given us new birth into a living hope through the resurrection of Jesus Christ from the dead." Through Jesus death and resurrection, we graduate to a new level in our life. We have a New Hope in life eternal with our Lord in heaven.

"Father, we thank and praise you for your great sacrifice. For sending your Son to die for our sins. Your mercy and grace surround us. We are proud to be your children. Amen"

Prayer Prompts:
Pray for grace and strength.
Pray for wisdom and peace.
Praise God for His guidance as we graduate each phase of our life.

Notes:

Use this page to write out your prayer...

54

HEALING

Healing can mean many things. We can need healing for an illness, a surgery, a loss, or even for a wrong done to us. For all of these, we start with prayer. God will give us strength to overcome whatever has caused us pain.

Matthew 9:35," Jesus *went through all the towns and villages, teaching in their synagogues, proclaiming the good news of the kingdom and healing every disease and sickness." Matthew 14:36, "and begged him to let the sick just touch the edge of his cloak, and all who touched it were healed."*

The power of Faith is enormous. We just have to believe, and God will work miracles in and for us. *Psalm 30:2, "Lord my God, I called to you for help, and you healed me." Luke 9:1-2 "When Jesus had called the Twelve together, he gave them power and authority to drive out all demons and to cure diseases, and* HE SENT THEM OUT *to preach the kingdom of God and* TO HEAL THE SICK.*"*

Through the Holy Spirit, God gives us the same powers he bestowed upon the disciples. Not everyone has the same gift of the Spirit, but some are granted the gift of healing. These gifts are explained in 1 Corinthians 12:4. We may not all be able to physically heal others, but we all have the power of prayer to ask God to help in the healing process.

"Lord Jesus, hear my prayer. Today I bring you the sick and oppressed. I lift them up and ask for your healing power over them. And lord, I especially bring you _____, fill in the name of who you are praying for. Help him/her to turn over their pain to you, so that you can bring them healing and peace. Amen."

Prayer Prompts:
Who do you know that is in the hospital?
A friend or coworker home sick from work?
Has anyone you know suffered a loss?
Pray for undernourished children all over the globe.
Pray for clean water for families all over the globe.

Notes:

Use this page to write out your prayer...

HOLY GROUND

Acts 7:33, Then the Lord said to him "take off the sandals from your feet, for the place where you are standing is holy ground."

Exodus 3:5, then he said, "do not come near; take your sandals off your feet, for the place on which you are standing is holy ground."

Joshua 5:15, and the commander of the Lord's army said to Joshua, "take off your sandals from your feet, for the place where you are standing is holy." and Joshua did so.

Taking off one's shoes was and still is a sign of reverence, humility, and respect. God certainly deserves all those things. So, what makes ground holy? The ground itself is not holy. It is the presence of God that makes it holy.

According to Wikipedia, holy means "associated with God." So, wherever you are in the presence of God, be reverent and show respect, you are standing on holy ground. If we want to take it a step further, the Holy Spirit is within us, so everywhere we go is holy. We should always be respectful of our actions and words. We are God's temple and we should show others through our actions, what it means to be a Christian.

"We are here in your presence Lord, standing in awe of you. Your spirit is in us, guiding us and teaching us every day. We praise you for all you have done for us. We thank you for the little things that we don't always think to say, the birds, the trees, all your creations. Amen"

Prayer Prompts:
Thank God for all the little day to day things in your life
Pray adoration: list God's attributes and praise him for them
Where do you feel God leading your life?
What steps can you take to share God with others?

Notes:

Use this page to write out your prayer...

IDOLS

Any image, statue, or good luck charm is a modern-day Idol. Some even idolize people. Celebrities, athletes, and musicians are a good example of this. God has made it very clear that he is the One and Only. *Exodus 20:3-4, You have no other gods before me. You shall not make for yourself an Idol in the form of anything in heaven above or on the earth beneath or in the waters below.*

Remember Charlton Heston in the Ten Commandments? Who hasn't seen this classic where Moses comes down the mountain with the stone tablets? The epic scene where he finds the people had made a golden Idol while he was gone? He heaves the heavy stone tablets at the idle and it bursts into flames.

There are several instances in the Bible that idols play a big role. One example is when Jacob takes his family and is finally moving away from their father's lands. *Genesis 31:34, Now Rachel had taken the household gods and put them inside her camel's saddle and was sitting on them. Laban searched through everything in the tent but found nothing.*

Another instance is King David's wife, Michal. She had taken a large idol from her father's house. Both of these women are married to prominent Christian men but cannot seem to give up the idols they grew up with. We cannot serve more than one God. *Leviticus 26:1, DO not make idols or set up an image or a sacred stone for yourselves, and do not place a carved stone in your land to bow down before it. I am the Lord your God.*

"Lord, I praise your Holy Name. I bow down and worship you, and only you, as my Almighty God. I will shout it from the mountain tops that you are God. Amen."

Prayer Prompt:
Pray that God will help you look only to Him
Pray for all the people out there that are unsure of God's Glory
Pray that God will remind us that celebrities are just people

Notes:

Use this page to write out your prayer...

IMMANUEL

Immanuel is just one of the many names of Jesus. In the Christmas song, O Come, O Come, Immanuel, we are reminded of God's promise to send us a Savior. The song reflects on the prophecy in Isaiah that foretold of the birth of Jesus Christ.

Isaiah 7:14, Therefore the Lord Himself will give you a sign: The virgin will be with child and will give birth to a son and will call him Immanuel. This promise is repeated in *Matthew 1:23, "The virgin will be with child and will give birth to a son, and they will call him Immanuel", - which means "God with us".*

This promise was given by God in the midst of all his anger with Sodom and Gomorrah. In the first few chapters of Isaiah, we find a very angry God. Isaiah warns the people to turn from sin or face God's wrath. Despite His anger with Israel, God gives Isaiah a promise for a better future.

Isaiah 9:6 For to us a child is born, to us a son is given, and the government will be on his shoulders. And he will be called "Wonderful Counselor, Mighty God, Everlasting Father, Prince of peace."

All of these names given to Jesus, define the roles of God, and remind us that Jesus and God are one in the same. Wonderful counselor, God is King and is in charge of our daily life. Mighty God, He will fight every battle for his people. Everlasting Father refers to His role as our provider and protector. And Prince of Peace shows that God is able to bring restoration to our lives.

"God is with us! Immanuel, King of Kings. Lord, we look to you for all our needs. We thank you for everything you do for us, for looking out for us, and fighting for us. Some days our battles are more than we can face, but we are never alone. You are always with us! Amen."

Prayer prompts:
Our Father has many roles. Pray for all aspects of your life.
Wonderful Counselor: Guide me Lord, help me to make all the right decisions today.
Mighty God: Lead the fight Lord, I cannot face the battles alone.
Everlasting Father: Guard my heart Jesus, I ask for your protection from evil.
Price of Peace: Restore a peace in my life and keep my Faith strong.

Notes:

Use this page to write out your prayer...

JOHN

Luke 1:13, But the Angel said to him, "do not be afraid, Zechariah, for your prayer has been heard, and your wife Elizabeth will bear you a son, and you shall call his name John. We all know how this story goes, Zechariah and Elizabeth are very old, well past childbearing age. God had made them a promise and he always keeps his promises. And *what an honor for them, the man their son would grow to be.*

Matthew 3:1 "In those days John the Baptist came preaching in the wilderness of Judea. Mark 1:4, John appeared, baptizing in the wilderness, and proclaiming a baptism of repentance for the forgiveness of sins.

God sent John to go forth and preach of the coming Messiah. To prepare the people for the birth of Christ. To baptize with water, so Jesus can follow baptizing in the Holy Spirit. *Matthew 11:11, "Truly I say to you, among those born of women there has arisen no one greater than John the Baptist. Yet the one who is least in the Kingdom of heaven is greater than he."*

John said it best himself. John 1:26-27, "I baptize with water", John replied, "but among you stands one you do not know. He is the one who comes after me, the thongs of whose sandals I am not worthy to untie."

John's purpose here on earth was to prepare the people for Jesus. As mothers, our purpose, is to prepare our children for Jesus. To teach them of God's love so they can grow to be strong men and women of faith. We must teach by example. Read our Bible daily, teach our children the import-ance of prayer, and to show forgiveness, as God has shown us daily.

"Lord, give me the wisdom of John. To know what your plan is for me here on earth. Guide me to do your work and bless all who assist me. I praise and adore your Holy name. Amen"

Prayer Prompts:
Pray for guidance in training up your children
Pray for friends and family who stand beside you
Pray for Christians of other countries where being baptized could get them killed

Notes:

Use this page to write out your prayer...

JOY

Psalm 94:19, "When anxiety was great within me, your consolation brought joy to my soul." The definition of joy is a feeling of great pleasure and happiness. I'd like to say that we all feel that way most of the time, but reality is that anxiety and stress are more the "norm" for most.

My suggestion? Turn on some worship music and turn off the news. There is nothing good going on out there. I can tell you that I am writing this as a mother of a high school senior who is missing prom and graduation because of the COVID19 virus. (As you are reading this in the future, it is April 2020, and the world is pretty much at a standstill.) So, stress and anxiety are real! But we Christians know where to find our JOY!

Psalm 47:1-2, Clap your hands, all you nations; shout to God with cries of joy. How awesome is the Lord Most High, the great King over all the earth!

Now, close your eyes and picture your "happy place". It could be a beach, a mountain cabin, or picture yourself in the middle of Eden. Surrounded by the most beautiful garden you can imagine. This is joy!

Romans 15:13, May the God of hope fill you with all the joy and peace as you trust in Him, so that you may overflow with hope by the power of the Holy Spirit.

In those moments when you start to feel everything pressing in, go to your happy place, take a few deep breaths, and ask God to fill you with joy and peace.

"Heavenly Father clear my mind of all the clutter. Bring me a sense of joy, that only you can. Take away all of the stresses and anxiety that have festered there. I ask this in the name of your Son, Jesus. Amen."

Prayer Prompts:
Pray for God to give you Joy.
Your family
Friends
Co-workers
Church Family

Notes:

Use this page to write out your prayer...

KINDNESS

Proverbs 21:21, "Whoever pursues righteousness and kindness will find life, righteousness, and honor." If you want to be treated with kindness, be kind. "Carry out a random act of kindness, with no expectation of reward, safe in the knowledge that one day someone might do the same for you." Princess Diana.

Wouldn't life be so much better if everyone could just be kind to each other. To do things to truly help people, without expecting anything in return. The Greek word for kindness means useful. Kindness is an action, to be useful to others. *Ephesians 4:32, Be kind to one another, tenderhearted, forgiving one another, as God in Christ forgave you.*

What if we all woke up each day and clothed ourselves in kindness, as in Colossians 3:12? What if we chose to be kind, to purposely do a random act of kindness? How many times have we heard of people paying for the car behind them in the drive-through or buying coffee for the next person in line?

Has anyone done that for you? There are so many ways to show kindness. You could find an organization in your area that needs volunteers, make sandwiches for the homeless, or mow your neighbor's lawn.

Start with your church. There are so many opportunities to help there. Greet people at the door, pass the communion tray, or if you are really brave, teach a Sunday School class. Start with something small and just see how it makes you feel.

"Lord, help me to help others. To be useful to those in need. To show others the kindness you have shown me through your son Jesus. Amen."

Prayer Prompts:
Pray for courage to take that first step toward helping others.
Pray for God to show you opportunities to be "useful".

Notes:

Use this page to write out your prayer...

KNEEL

When we kneel or bow before God, we are showing respect. We are humbled and submissive to our Almighty Father. *"Psalm 95:6, Come let us bow down in worship, let us kneel before the Lord our maker."*

We learn at a young age to kneel beside our bed when we say our prayers. We fold our hands and bow our heads to give God our full attention. Even Jesus bowed in respect when praying to the Father. *Luke 22:41, and he withdrew from them about a stone's throw, and knelt down and prayed.*

In the movie "War Room", Miss Clara turned her walk-in closet into a place of prayer. She would go there to be alone with God. Kneeling down in her private place, she prayed in depth for everyone she knew. She even wrote out the prayers and hung them on the wall. A true "Prayer Warrior". In Jesus name...

Philippians 2:10, So that at the name of Jesus, every knee should bow, in heaven and on earth and under the earth. We should all find that special place where we can kneel before our Lord and give him our full attention.

Our Father in Heaven, hear my prayer...

Prayer Prompts:

Who do you need to pray for? Husband, child, sibling, friend? Take out a sheet of paper and write out your prayer. If you have never done this before, think of it as writing a letter to God. Tape it up somewhere where you can read it each day during your prayer time. Keep praying that same prayer as long as it is needed.

For example, I have a child heading off to college.

"Lord, I lift up my child to you. Wrap her in your protection. Give her grace and courage to face this new adventure. Guide her with wisdom to know when to walk away and give her perseverance to tackle her classes. Most of all Lord, remind her to do all things to your Glory, so that others will see You in her. Amen."

Notes:

Use this page to write out your prayer...

LEARNING TO PRAY

As children, we learn to memorize a table prayer or a bedtime prayer. For example, "Thank you Jesus for this food, and bless it to our bodies." Or, "Now I lay me down to sleep..." usually followed by "God Bless", and a long list of friends and family. When we get older, we learn the Lord's prayer found in Matthew 6:9-13.

In Luke 11:1, one of Jesus disciples says "Lord, teach us to pray". Verse 2, "When you pray, say Father, hallowed be your name."

Slowly we learned to add a few requests, like, I sure would like a new bike, or "Jesus, please help me to..." You fill in the blank. Jeremiah 33:3, "Call to me and I will answer you and tell you great things you do not know." And Psalm 17:6, "I call on you, my God, for you will answer me: turn your ear to me and hear my prayer."

Getting started is as easy as talking to someone beside you. God is a loving Father. Just tell Him how you feel.

"Father God, thank you for all your guidance, for having a plan for me, and showing me the way. I praise your holy name. Lord, lift me up, and give me wisdom to know what is right, and what is wrong, and to go in the right direction. Amen."

Prayer Prompts:
Pray for your family members
Praise God for something good in your life
Pray for your Pastor

Notes:

Use this page to write out your prayer...

LOVE

Matthew 22: 37-39, Jesus replied, love the Lord your God with all your heart and with all your soul and with all your mind. This is the first and greatest commandment and the 2nd is like it; love your neighbor as yourself. Every mother has quoted this one… treat others as you want to be treated. That is the basis of what Jesus is saying in these verses. Be good to each other; love each other, like God is good and loving to us.

1 John 4:16, 19, And so we know and rely on the love God has for us. God is love. Whoever lives in love lives in God, and God in them. V19 We love because he first loved us.

Can you imagine how different the world would be if we all lived by this standard? Everyone treating each other with love and respect? John 15:12-13, My commandment is this: love each other as I have loved you. Greater love has no one than this, that he lay down his life for his friends. Romans 12:9, Love must be sincere. Hate what is evil; cling to what is good.

Pray to be sincere, that your actions speak louder than words. Let them know we are Christians by our love… as the song goes.

"Lord God, thank you for the greatest love you could share. Your Son, Jesus. Through Him, we have eternal life. Help us to love one another, as you love us. Amen."

Prayer Prompts:

Pray for all of your loved ones, that they will know our blessed savior, and that through His love, we will all be together in Heaven.

Notes:

Use this page to write out your prayer...

MARY

Reading through the gospels, we find a number of women who played a huge role in Jesus life, all named Mary. In fact, there are six of them. We'll begin in Matthew with Mary, Jesus mother. Not a lot is known about her, other than she is of the tribe of Judah, and from the line of David. In Matthew 1:18-23, we're told of the pregnant virgin and her betrothed Joseph. In John, chapter 2, we find Mary instructing Jesus to perform his first miracle where he turns water into wine at the wedding in Cana.

Next, we have Mary Magdalene. Jesus healed her of demon possession, and we are told she was a wealthy supporter of his early ministry. Mary Magdalene was also the first to see the Risen Lord!

Mary of Bethany, sister of Lazarus and Martha. We find her in *John 12:3, Then Mary took about a pint of pure nard, an expensive perfume; she poured it on Jesus feet and wiped his feet with her hair. And the house was filled with the fragrance of the perfume.*

Standing at the foot of the cross, we find another Mary. Mary, wife of Clopas, and sister in law to Jesus mother. This Mary plays a supporting role by holding up his mother at the cross, alongside Mary Magdalene. *John 19:25, Near the cross of Jesus stood his mother, his mother sister, (Mary the wife of Clopas), and Mary Magdalene.*

Mary, mother of Mark, supported Jesus by supplying a meeting place. Her home is where the Last Supper took place. In *Acts 12:12, Peter goes to the house of Mary, the mother of John, also called Mark, where many people had gathered and were praying.*

We don't know much about our 6th Mary. She was introduced by Paul as someone who "labored much" for those serving the church. *Romans 16:6, Greet Mary, who worked very hard for you.*

"Lord, we thank you for showing us these remarkable women. We strive to be like them, to show our Faith through our actions. Lord, I thank you for making me the strong woman I am today. Amen."

Prayer Prompts:
Pray for wisdom to know how and when can show who we are in Christ.

Notes:

Use this page to write out your prayer...

MIRACLES

Who can tell me the first miracle Jesus performed? I'll give you a hint... His momma made him do it. In John 2:1-11, we read about the wedding at Cana where Jesus turned water into wine.

Or read Matthew 14:19-21, where Jesus feeds a crowd of 5000 people with two fish and five loaves of bread. There are a number of times that Jesus healed the sick.

Matthew 8:2-3, A man with leprosy came and knelt before him and said, "Lord if you are willing, you can make me clean". Jesus reached out his hand and touched the man. "I am willing." He said. "Be clean"! Immediately he was cured of his leprosy.

And even better, Jesus brought Lazarus back from the dead in John 11:40-44. *(43) Jesus called in a loud voice. "Lazarus come out!", and he did.*

We have all seen or at least heard of some modern-day miracles. Every time a baby is born, or someone is cured of cancer, that is a miracle. Something as small as planting a seed and watching a flower grow, that too is a miracle.

.   Every day God shows us something wonderful. We just need to be looking.

"Lord, everywhere I look, I see the wonders of your mighty hand. I ask that you keep my eyes on you Lord. Don't let me miss out on the miracles you have to offer. Amen."

Prayer prompts:
Pray for friends and family to see all that God has to offer.
Pray for God's glory to show itself in your life.

Notes:

Use this page to write out your prayer...

NARROW GATE

Matthew 7:13, "Enter through the narrow gate. For wide is the gate and broad is the road that leads to destruction, and many enter through it but small is the gate and narrow the road that leads to life, and only a few find it." Jesus is waiting at the narrow gate to give us life eternal. Stand strong in your faith and you too, will be welcomed through the gate. Even more important, share your faith. God asked us all to go forward as disciples and spread the word. Share your experiences and beliefs.

Matthew 28:19-20, "Go and make disciples of all nations, baptizing them in the name of the father, and the son, and of the Holy Spirit, teaching them to observe all that I have commanded you."

That is our commandment, to go out into the world and share our God. When we *all head toward the gate, we want to have helped lead many others there as well.*

Luke 13:24, Strive to enter through the narrow gate. For many, I tell you, will seek to enter and will not be able.

"Lord, thank you for loving us and guiding us, for leading us toward the narrow gate. Even

when we walk through the Valley, you are with us.
You are our light. Amen."

Prayer Prompts:
Pray that the Lord guide you to the gate, that you
may show others the way.

Notes:

Use this page to write out your prayer...

NUMBERS

In numbers, we learn that the first census took place a long time ago. God instructed Moses and Aaron to count the clans and families of Israel. I work in accounting and like numbers, but stats are not my thing, until now. I find it fascinating that such precise records were kept so long ago.

I had no idea how many slaves followed Moses to the desert. The movie doesn't give an accurate picture of the masses. When God split the sea, it wasn't for a few minutes to get 5000 or 10,000 people to safety. It had to take hours to get the over 600,000 people across. This gives us just a glimpse of God's power.

Numbers 2:32, These are the Israelites, counted according to their families. All those in the camps, by their divisions, number 603,550.

The book of numbers goes on to give very descriptive instructions for the Israelites. When to pick up camp, and when to stay. What to eat, where to set up camp, and which family is in charge of what. Through it all God provides for his people. He also brings the wrath when needed. The Lord expects us to follow his instructions explicitly.

Numbers 11:1, Now the people complained about their hardships in the hearing of the Lord, and when He heard them His anger was aroused.

God promised His people a land of milk and honey. Time after time, He provided food and water. Still the people rebelled. We are the same today as the Israelites so long ago. We whine and complain when things don't go the way we expect. God wants a relationship with us, not just someone who calls on him in time of need. He wants our praise and worship, and to thank him for the good as well.

"God, we appreciate all you have done for us. We ask that you forgive us for the sins we have sinned against you by not listening when you speak. We ask that you open our ears to hear your voice. We repent the times we stray from your path or complain when things don't go our way. Amen."

Prayer Prompts:
Pray for God's blessings over your family
Praise God for creation
Pray for God's attribute of love

Notes:

Use this page to write out your prayer...

OMNISCIENT

The meaning of omniscient, is having infinite awareness, understanding, and insight, complete knowledge.

As a mother, have you ever wished you had eyes in the back of your head? Come on, we've all said it. God, He sees everything.

Hebrews 4:13, And no creature is hidden from His sight, but all are naked and exposed to the eyes of Him to whom we must give account. Proverbs 15:3, The eyes of the Lord are in every place, keeping watch on the evil and the good.

God is the Shepherd, always watching over his flock. He is our Guardian and protector.

Job 28:24, For He looks to the ends of the earth and sees everything under the heavens. Job 34:21, For His eyes are on the ways of a man, and He sees all his steps.

Our God is an awesome God. He has a purpose and a plan for each of His children. He will guide us on our journey if we just let Him. *Matthew 6:8b, for your Father knows what you need before you ask Him.*

But don't be afraid to ask. God wants us to need Him. He is our father in heaven and He loves all his children.

"Our Father in heaven, hear our prayer. We love you and we glorify your name. You are a loving Father of whom we adore. Thank you for all the blessings you provide. Amen."

Prayer Prompts:
Pray for parental guidance
Pray love over your children
Pray blessings over family and friends
Pick 1 person you haven't talked to in a while and pray in depth for their physical and spiritual health

Notes:

Use this page to write out your prayer...

99

OPEN THE DOOR

Revelations 3:20, "Behold, I stand at the door and knock. If anyone hears my voice and opens the door, I will come into him and eat with him, and he with me."

If Jesus knocked on your door today, would you be ready? Would you invite Him in for a Cup of coffee? How amazing it would have been to have sat with Him in the upper room. To break bread and hear His stories in person. We can all have that personal relationship with Jesus.

Just ask Him into your heart. Pray to Him like He's sitting next to you. An open conversation with our Lord is an amazing thing. Praise Him and thank Him, then sit quietly and listen. You will be amazed at what you might hear.

Matthew 7:7, Ask and it will be given to you; seek and you will find; knock, and it will be opened to you.

"Jesus, I welcome you into my heart, my home, my life. Thank you for being my guide, protector, and lifeline. For giving me an eternal life through your death. I praise your Holy name! You are my light in the darkness. Amen."

Prayer Prompts:
For Jesus to make a home in your heart.
To give you a calm and peace that you can meditate and hear what he has to say.
To give your life over to His guidance.
To have that personal relationship that enables you to talk to Him like he's a friend in the room.

Notes:

Use this page to write out your prayer...

PRAISE

Do you have a favorite worship song? I could fill a whole page just trying to decide. When you are standing in church Sunday morning, is there a particular song that brings tears to your eyes? Or one that makes you want to start praise dancing in the aisles? Praise is an emotional part of worshipping our God. *Psalm 149:3, Let them praise His name with dancing and make music to Him with tambourine and harp. Psalm 150:6, Let everything that has breath praise the Lord. Praise the Lord.*

I Chronicles 16:9, Sing to Him, sing praise to Him; tell of all His wonderful acts.

To give praise is to take action. To dance and sing before the Lord. Lift up your hands or get down on your knees. How you praise is only up to you. Take action and show God what He means in your life. David danced before the Lord basically in his underwear..." undignified", as found in 2 Samuel 6:20.

When David returned home to bless his household, Michal daughter of Saul came out to meet him and said, "How the king of Israel has distinguished himself today, going around half-naked in full view of the slave girls of his servants as any vulgar fellow would!"

"Praise our Lord in any way you wish, sing, dance, shout from the mountains...

"Lord, I lift up my praise and worship your Holy name. You are the King of Kings! Way Maker, Miracle Worker, ... Amen"

Prayer Prompts:
Do you have a praise report? New job, new baby in the family, Newly married family member or friend? Is there an upcoming event you are looking forward to? Or just give thanks for all the blessings in your life.

Notes:

Use this page to write out your prayer...

105

PRAYING FROM THE HEART

We have all had moments where we offer up a quick prayer of thanks. Those times when you're driving to work, singing along at the top of your lungs… and suddenly, the car in front of you slams on their brakes. You swerve, just miss them, and quickly glance toward Heaven and thank the Lord for His protection. Or, you're having a rough morning. The kids are running late for school, the toast is burning, and you remember it's potluck day at work. You close your eyes, "Lord, grant me patience and wisdom to get through this day."

Psalm 18:6," In my distress I called to the Lord; I cried to my God for help" These are minuscule examples of prayer. Philippians 4:6 tells us why we should pray. *"Do not be anxious about anything, but in everything, by prayer and petition, with thanksgiving, present your requests to God."* Matthew 6:6, *"But when you pray, go into your room, close the door and pray to your Father, who is unseen. Then your Father, who sees what is done in secret, will reward you."*

So, here we are, alone on our knees ready to open our hearts to our Loving Father.

"Father God, I thank and praise you for all

you've brought me through this day, week, month. I lift up songs of worship in your Holy Name. I ask you for guidance and wisdom into the next days to come, that I might follow the path you have so painstakingly laid out for me. I ask that…" Answer the few questions below to add to the prayer and personalize it. Prayer is a powerful tool. It is a way for us to support others as well as ourselves. It can fight illness, bring us joy, and even free us from demons. Amen"

Prayer Prompts:
Do I have any family members or friends in need?
Are any of my friends or family sick or hurt?
Any upcoming events?

Notes:

Use this page to write out your prayer...

QUEEN ESTHER

In the book of Esther, we have 10 chapters that read like a novel. Current Queen Vashti makes the King angry and gets herself banished. (Better than beheaded) Then, the King's *personal attendants gather all the beautiful virgins in the land, so he can pick a new Queen. Esther 2:17, Now the King was attracted to Esther more than any of the other women, and she won his favor and approval more than any of the other virgins. So, he set a Royal Crown on her head and made her Queen instead of Vashti.*

Next, Esther's cousin, Mordecai, learns of a plot to kill the King. He tells Esther so she can inform the King. The two plotting the attack were hanged, and Haman was promoted to "right hand man".

Haman doesn't like Mordecai and gets a degree passed to kill the Jews. He even has gallows built in his own yard for Mordecai. Short version here, Esther pleads with the King to spare her people and reveals she is a Jew. *Esther 7:3, Then Queen Esther answered, if I have found favor with you, O King, and if it pleases your Majesty, grant me my life, this is my petition. And spare my people, this is my request.*

The King, angry at Haman, declares he be

hung on the same gallows he had built for Mordecai. *Esther 7:10, So they hanged Haman on the gallows he had prepared for Mordecai. Then the King's fury subsided.*

King Xerxes promoted Mordecai to Haman's vacated position. Esther 10:3, Mordecai the Jew was second in rank to King Xerxes, preeminent among the Jews, and held in high esteem by his many fellow Jews, because he worked for the good of his people and spoke up for the welfare of all Jews.

Esther's bravery to speak up and confront Haman in front of the King, saved her people. In those days, a woman was not always listened to, and because of that she took a big risk. Esther knew that God was right there beside her. He would never forsake his people.

"Dear Lord in Heaven, thank you for always listening and hearing our prayers, for looking out for us, and showing us your grace and mercy. Lord, guide us and show us your will for our lives, that we can show others your great mercy. Amen."

Prayer Prompts:
Help us to always stand up for what is right, to combat evil, and live by example.

Notes:

Use this page to write out your prayer...

QUIET

The definition of quiet is the absence of noise or bustle; silence; calm. In the Bible we find that Jesus often looked for quiet places to be alone and pray. *Mark 1:35, Before Daybreak the next morning, Jesus got up and went out to an isolated place to pray. Luke 5:16, But Jesus often withdrew to lonely places and prayed.*

For us, that could be in our car driving to work, in the shower, or kneeling beside the bed before going to sleep. I'd like to share a quote from author Marilyn Meberg. She said, "no one is born with a personal relationship with God, we must ask for it."

Prayer is an intimate time with God. Start by finding a time to share with Him on a personal level. Begin by praising Him and move on to praying for others in need. Some people like to make a list. Write down all your family and friends, then note their needs or praises. A family member may need prayers for a recent medical diagnosis or praise for a wedding or new baby. Making a list ensures nothing gets left out. Pray for your local and national politicians, health care workers, and first responders.

You can also use this quiet time for meditation. Read your Bible and reflect on the passages. I like to start my quiet time with a devotional and reflect on its meaning.

No matter the topic, I can usually find a connection in my own life. Then I pray. I bare my soul to my Savior and ask His forgiveness and guidance before praying for friends and family. It's easy to get started, just talk to God like He were a friend sitting in the chair next to you.

"Father God, I reflect on the glory of this day. I admire your creations all around me. It restores my soul to see all that you have done. To just sit in the quiet and breathe. To know you are with me in the silence calms me. Amen."

Prayer Prompts:
Pray for God to sit with you in your quiet place, and then just listen.
Sit in quiet reflection.
Pray for a calm over your life.

Notes:

Use this page to write out your prayer...

RAINBOW

Next time it rains, look up at the clouds and you may spot a rainbow. In this story, there is no pot of gold and no leprechaun. This rainbow is a promise from God. *Genesis 9:13, I have set my rainbow in the clouds, and it will be the sign of the covenant between me and the earth.*

You see, if we back up to the beginning of the story, we find Noah building a very large boat in the middle of the desert. "Why?" you ask. *Genesis 6:5, 8 The Lord saw how great man's wickedness on the earth had become and that every inclination of the thoughts of his heart was only evil all the time...8 but Noah found favor in the eyes of the Lord.*

God told Noah there was going to be a great flood, and told him to build an Ark. The instructions were very specific, and Noah followed them exactly. When God said to get on the boat, Noah, and his family, along with two of every animal boarded the boat, and the rain began.

Genesis 7:12, and rain fell on the earth forty days and forty nights. Genesis 7:24, the waters flooded the earth for one hundred and fifty days. When the waters receded, Noah and his family were all that remained.

God made a promise to Noah that the earth

would never be destroyed by flood again. He placed a rainbow in the clouds as a reminder of that promise. Genesis 9:15b-16a Never again will the waters become a flood to destroy all life. Whenever the rainbow appears in the clouds, I will see it and remember the everlasting covenant.

"Father, we praise you for all you have given us. For creating us and providing all the plants and animals to sustain us. You have blessed us through your covenant and given us the rainbow as a sign of your commitment to us. We commit ourselves to you and worship your Holy Name. Amen."

Prayer Prompts:
Give thanks to God for all he has given you.
Praise Him for the heavens and the earth.
Ask for guidance to stay on a path of righteousness and to keep you from evil.

Notes:

Use this page to write out your prayer...

RESILIENCE

Able to withstand or recover quickly from difficult conditions. *Psalm 50:15, "Pray to me when you are in trouble! I will deliver you and you will honor me! "*

There are a number of instances in the Bible where times are tough. Daniel faced the lion. Shadrack, Meshach, and Abednego lived through the fiery furnace. What about Jonah? He spent three days in the belly of a whale. With God's help, Christians can endure anything. He will help us through.

Joshua 1:9, I repeat, be strong and brave! Don't be afraid and don't panic, for I, the Lord your God, am with you in all you do. Our heavenly father has a plan and purpose for each and every one of his children.

Trust in the Lord your God. Pray for Him to strengthen your faith each morning and praise Him for His glory as you settle in for the night. *Jeremiah 29:11, For I know the plans I have for you - this is the Lord's declaration - plans for your welfare, not for disaster, to give you a future and a hope.*

We all have faced turmoil. How we handle it determines our future. Look to God to keep you strong, to wage war for you, and to keep you strong in your faith. I am in that place right now! It has not been easy and sometimes you just want to give up. But I am telling you from my heart, that prayer works!

"Lord, I know you are there for me. You hold me up when I just want to fall. You are the steps in the sand when I just can't walk anymore. You are my rock and my protection. I praise your Holy Name. Amen."

Prayer Prompts:
What you put here is going to depend on who is in turmoil at present. Is it you, a family member, a friend? Maybe a boss or coworker. No matter who is hurting, your prayers can be a mighty power to help them hold it together. Pray long and pray continually. God will hear you. He is always listening.

Notes:

Use this page to write out your prayer...

RETREAT

Retreat, to withdraw, also a refuge or sanctuary. So, what does it mean to go on retreat? It can mean a few different things. When our women's group goes on "retreat", it is a time to worship and reflect on our savior. As an individual, we may seek a quiet place of refuge to read our Bible and pray in solitude. To spend time alone with Christ.

Psalm 46:1, "God is our refuge and strength." Refuge is defined as being safe or sheltered. Taking refuge in God means finding complete safety in him. *"Psalm 31:2, turn your ear to me, come quickly to my rescue; be my rock of refuge, a strong fortress to save me."*

It is good to take a retreat from your everyday routine. A weekend with just you and Jesus. Dig deep into his word and give praise for all the blessings you have received. Even an hour of your day alone with your devotions and prayers, is a time of retreat. Time we dedicate to our Lord in return for all the refuge he provides to us.

On a personal note, if your church has a women's retreat, GO! It can be an amazing opportunity to form close relationships with other women in your church, and better yet, it will enhance your personal relationship with God.

"Retreat" to a quiet place to be alone with Jesus. Take time to pray, truly pray, an in-depth conversation with our Savior. Seek sanctuary in His presence. Pray for a peace that only he can give.

"Father, we seek refuge in your embrace. We thank you for giving us a safe place to worship Your name. So many in other countries are not as lucky. We pray for their safety as they worship you in the dark of night. We pray your protection over them, and all your children. Amen."

Prayer Prompts:
Pray for other nations to witness our Father's love.
Pray for refuge for those in danger of persecution.
Pray for light in the darkness.

Notes:

Use this page to write out your prayer...

SALVATION

Isaiah 12:2, Surely God is my Salvation; I will trust and not be afraid. The Lord, the Lord is my strength and my song, He has become my Salvation. In short, Salvation means deliverance from harm. God has delivered us from evil through the precious blood of Christ. *Acts 2:12, And everyone who calls on the name of the Lord will be saved.*

What an amazing gift God has given all of us who believe in His son. At churches we celebrate communion as a remembrance of the blood Jesus shed for each and every believer. That we should not perish but have eternal life.

Matthew 26:26-28, While they were eating, Jesus took bread, gave thanks and broke it, and gave it to his disciples, saying, "take and eat; this is my body". Then he took the cup, gave thanks and offered it to them, saying, "drink from it all of you"

Shortly after sharing this with his disciples, Jesus began the three-day journey to our Salvation. He died, was buried, and rose again. Through Jesus, God has forgiven all our sins. He is our Salvation.

Psalm 62:1, Truly my soul finds rest in God; my Salvation comes from him.
Titus 2:11, For the grace of God that brings Salvation has appeared to all men.

"Lord, thank you for your Son, for His body and blood that purifies us. We praise you for all you do to keep us safe, for giving us your Salvation, and keeping us from evil. Amen."

Prayer prompts:
Pray for all the unbelievers, that they will see the light and believe in God's Salvation.

Notes:

Use this page to write out your prayer...

STRENGTH

The Lord is our strength. He is there any time we need Him, even when we don't realize it. *Psalm 46:1, God is our refuge and strength, an ever-present help in trouble. Isaiah 40:29, He gives power to the weak and strength to the powerless.*

When you find yourself stressed or worried, call out the name of Jesus. As the song says, "there's power in the name". I've been known to look to the heavens and yell "Jesus, Jesus, Jesus".

Next, PRAY! Ask for God's mercy and His help. Prayer is powerful. Ask friends and family to pray for you, or with you. There is strength in numbers, the more prayer warriors you have in your corner, the better. I can assure you; I have lived that first hand.

Isaiah 41:10, So do not fear, for I am with you; do not be dismayed, for I am your God. I will strengthen you and help you; I will uphold you with my righteous right hand.

Our God is a powerful God. He wants us, His children, to live and prosper. No father wants to see his children suffer. Ask and you shall receive... *Matthew 7:7, Ask and it shall be given you; seek and you shall find; knock, and it shall be opened unto you.* God wants us to seek Him out, to ask for His help.

All fathers want to be needed they want their children to know they can always come to them for anything.

1 Chronicles 16:11, Look to the Lord and his strength; seek his face always.

"God, we do seek you. We seek your mercy and strength. We need you Father in good times and bad. Help us to follow the path You have chosen for us. To not let this world side-track us from Your Will in our lives. Amen."

Prayer Prompts:
Pray Psalm 46:1
Let God be your refuge and strength. Give Him your burdens to carry. In the roughest of times, remember... the one set of footprints in the sand are God's, because He is carrying you!

Notes:

Use this page to write out your prayer...

SURROUNDED

"It may look like I'm surrounded, but I'm Surrounded by you!" In the song Surrounded by Upper Room, we are reminded that no matter what we are facing, God is there.

Psalm 5:12, "God surrounds and protects me with favor like a shield!" No matter how dark our day may be, God is with us, walking beside us. And as the poem "Footprints" points out, at our worst of times He carries us. Always protecting us and shielding us from evil. That is not to say that evil cannot reach us, just that God will help us through whatever situation we may face.

Psalm 33:22, "Let your unfailing love surround us Lord, for our hope is in you alone." Our Lord is our hope, our Salvation, He holds out His hand and guides us. We may not know where we're going, but Jesus does. Our lives were planned before we were born. God has it all mapped out, but that does not mean that there won't be hurdles along the way. Free Will can get us in trouble every time. We have to believe in God's promises and want to follow His path. If we choose to take the wrong fork in the road, He will not forsake us. He will still help guide us toward the right path.

Deuteronomy 31:8, "It is the Lord who goes be-

fore you. He will be with you; He will not leave you or
forsake you. Do not fear or be dismayed."

Remember in the worst of times, when life seems overwhelming and you feel surrounded, God's love is surrounding you. "It may look like I'm surrounded, but I'm surrounded by you!"

"Lord God, we praise you for all your glory. You are with us in the best of times and carry us through the worst. Thank you for surrounding us in your love and protection. You are our light in the darkness. Amen."

Prayer Prompts:
Thank God for surrounding you with His glory.
Praise Him for always having your back.
Pray for courage in the storm.

Notes:

Use this page to write out your prayer...

TRUMPETS

Trumpets are a big deal in the Bible. In Joshua 6:1-27, we learn how Jericho fell. God told the army to march around the city once each day for six days, then seven times on the 7th day, followed by a blast of trumpets. The result? The walls came tumbling down. Can you imagine the surprise on everyone's faces? Our God is a mighty God! In Numbers, God tells his people other times they should sound the trumpet.

Numbers 10:2, "Make two trumpets of hammered silver and use them for calling the community together and for having the camps set out." *Numbers 10:10, "Also at your times of rejoicing - you're appointed festival's and new moon feasts - you are to sound the trumpets over your burnt offerings and fellowship offerings, and they will be a memorial for you before your God. I am the Lord your God."*

Next time you want to call the family to dinner, break out the trumpet. Dust it off and give it a blast. Praise our Lord with trumpets. Music has always been a big part of worship and as we see here, it goes all the way back to the Old Testament. Psalm 98:6, "With trumpets and the blast of a Rams horn - shout for joy before the Lord, the King!

"Father God, you are a mighty God! Let the trumpets sound to celebrate your glory. We praise you Lord for all the victories you have given your people. You led us out of darkness and into the light. We praise your Holy name. Amen."

Prayer prompts:
Thank God for your personal victories
Ask Him to lead you through your next battle
Praise Him for bringing you out from the darkness

Notes:

Use this page to write out your prayer...

TRUTH

John 14:6, Jesus answered, "I am the way and the truth and the life. No one comes to the Father except through me." Jesus is our truth. He is our guide through the path of life, and death. He is our way to our Father in Heaven.

3 John 1:4, I have no greater joy than to hear that my children are walking in the truth. This means, walking with Jesus. Or even bigger picture, walking a Godly life.

The Bible is God's Truth, written by disciples and other great historians so that we will know God and can follow Jesus. Ephesians 4:15, *Instead, speaking the truth in love, we will grow to become in every respect the mature body of him who is the head, that is, Christ. 1 John 3:18, Dear children, let us not love with words or speech but with actions and in truth.*

We cannot just say we are Christians. We must act in a way that shows the world we are Christians. A Christian should not lie, or cheat, or swear. He should love and show mercy and live in Truth. The devil will always put people in our path to test us. We need to stay strong in God. Praise Him and worship Him, and pray daily to Him, and he will show us what is true.

"Father God, I ask that you hold me up and keep me strong. Help me to be true to your Word. Guide my steps as I continue my walk of faith. I lift praises in Jesus name. Amen"

Prayer Prompts:
Pray for other Christians, family, and friends, that they will walk with Jesus
Pray for our world leaders to live in Truth
Pray that you will stand strong through any test and trials that my come your way

Notes:

Use this page to write out your prayer...

UNATTAINABLE

With God, nothing is unattainable. In the book of Deuteronomy, God tells us, His people, He will give them life and prosperity, or they can choose death and destruction.

Deuteronomy 30:10-11, If you obey the Lord your God and keep His commands and decrees that are written in the book of the law and turn to the Lord your God with all your heart and all your soul. Indeed, these commands that I'm giving you today are neither confusing nor unattainable for you.

The simple truth is that loving our God with heart and soul will give us life and prosperity. Not just life on earth, but everlasting life with Him in heaven. What a glorious and gracious God. He wants what's best for us, just like what we want what's best for our family.

We want nothing to be unattainable for our children. We raise them up to love and honor God so that He will provide prosperity and life to them. We train and educate them and tell them they can do anything they set their minds to. We teach them to pray to our Heavenly Father to show them the path He has set for them, and we pray we've taught them well how to listen for His guidance.

"Lord, creator of life, hear our prayer. We thank you for all things you do for us that we do not even know about. Even when we don't see it, you are working to make our lives better. You are always watching and listening. You know what we need before we do. Praise you Father, Son, and Holy Spirit for the gifts you have bestowed on each one of us. Make it clear what you have planned for us to do. For with you Lord, nothing is unattainable. Amen."

Prayer Prompts:
Pray for your children. Sometimes they get out of hand, or maybe even fly the coop, but they are still our children. We love them unconditionally like God loves us. Pray for God to watch over them, protect them, and guide them. To help them discover their special gifts and use them to honor Him.

Notes:

Use this page to write out your prayer...

UNITY

Unity is when a group is joined for a common purpose or by a common feeling. As Christians, we are united in Christ. *Ephesians 4:3, "Make every effort to keep yourselves united in the spirit, binding yourselves together with peace."* Our church family and small groups are both groups united to keep us strong. *Matthew 18:20, For where two or three gathers in my name, there am I with them.*

Unity is an important part of our lives. Having people to "do" life with. People to show support in times of need and to cheer us on when reaching for new goals. "Our family", "Our village." *Malachi 2:10, Are we not all children of the same father? Are we not all created by the same God?* Like brothers and sisters, all with our own unique qualities and gifts. All united by one Holy Father who loved us so much he sent Jesus to die for our sins. We are all forgiven, given an empty slate.

Our unity in Christ puts us in a special class of people. *Peter 3:8, Finally all of you have unity of mind, sympathy, brotherly love, a tender heart, and a humble mind.* So, brothers and sisters stand tall, be strong, and show the world what it means to be a Christian.

"Lord we ask for wisdom as we face the world. We are your sons and daughters and want others to see that in our actions and speech. Help us to know when to speak, and when to listen. Guide us on our journey to bring new believers into the family of Christ. Amen."

Prayer Prompts:
Pray for a family member or friend who needs to know Jesus.
Ask God to guide you in teaching others about Jesus.
Pray for your "Village".

Notes:

Use this page to write out your prayer...

VICTORY

We must all choose our battles wisely, and our words carefully. But know this, when you have to fight, know that your faith will keep you strong. *Deuteronomy 20:4, For the Lord your God is the one who goes with you to fight for you against your enemies to give you victory.* In the song "Surrounded", by Upper Room, we are surrounded by God and this is how we fight our battles.

The song is based on *II Chronicles 20:17, You will not have to fight this battle. Take up your positions; stand firm and see the deliverance the Lord will give you, Judah, and Jerusalem. Do not be afraid; do not be discouraged. Go out to face them tomorrow, and the Lord will be with you.*

God will fight our battles; all he asks of us is to have faith. Do as God says and stand your ground. *Ephesians 6:13, Therefore put on the full armor of God, so that when the day of evil comes, you may be able to stand your ground, and after you have done everything, to stand.*

Need a good fight song? One of my favorites is" See A Victory" by Elevation Worship. "I'm going to see a victory for the battle belongs to you Lord." "You take what the enemy meant for evil and you turn it for good." *Proverbs 21:31, The horse is made ready for the day of battle but victory rests with the Lord.* Our God is a mighty warrior, stand tall and have faith!

"Heavenly Father, I kneel before you humbled by your presence. You are a mighty warrior, and I know that you fight for me every day. I praise and worship at your feet. You give my strength and wisdom. You have my undying devotion and my faith holds firm. Amen."

Prayer Prompts:
Pray for missionaries in countries where their lives are at risk every day. Pray for God to fight for them as they bring new Christians into the fold.
Pray for the worship leaders whose songs reach thousands. Let the words bring people closer to God.
Pray for your own battles. We are all in the midst of something. Pray for guidance and He will get you through.

Notes:

Use this page to write out your prayer...

VINEYARD

When we think vineyard, our first thought is wine, but it's way more complicated than that. Like anything worth striving for, it takes hard work and perseverance before that first bottle is poured. Prepare the soil, plant the vines, tend the vines, prune the vines, pick the fruit, I think you get the picture. It's hard work.

Proverbs 31:16, "She considers a field and buys it; with the fruit of her hands she plants a vineyard." In the end, the reward is worth the wait. Gather some friends, pop the Cork, and celebrate your success. You earned it.

Even here, "God is in the small stuff." In Deuteronomy, God uses a vineyard to provide for the less fortunate. Similar to how he provided for Ruth and Naomi in the fields.

Deuteronomy 24:21, "When thou gatherest the grapes of the vineyard, thou shalt not glean it afterward: it shall be for the stranger, for the fatherless, and for the widow."

God is telling us to look after the less fortunate. Through our churches and small groups, we know how important that support is when we have a need. People surround us with love, prayers, food, support, and more food. What is it about casseroles that make life seem a little better?

Okay, back to the wine. Pour a glass and enjoy a good book, or THEE GOOD BOOK. Remember, wine was just water until Jesus got his hands on it.

"Lord, you are with us in every little thing. We thank you for providing for us and giving us the opportunity to provide help to others. Praise you for the blessings you bestow upon us. Your glory and mercy surround us and keep us safe. Amen."

Prayer Prompts:
To give us courage to step out in faith to help others in need
To provide us with knowledge and wisdom
To give God the glory, not ourselves
Praise God for the "small stuff"

Notes:

Use this page to write out your prayer...

WARRIORS

I could tell you about many great Warriors throughout the Bible, such as David fighting Goliath or Israel marching on Jericho. But today I want to focus on Prayer Warriors. If you've ever experienced the true power of prayer, you'll know what I mean. A Prayer Warrior is anyone who is committed to praying for others. And where two or more gather, the results can be life changing.

Acts 1:14, "All these with one accord or devoting themselves to prayer, together with women and Mary the mother of Jesus, and his brothers.

I have experienced this power personally. Both as a recipient of such prayers, and as a warrior myself. A small example is a group all praying for you during a job interview, or even a surgery. The presence of God is so strong that you can feel Him in the room. What employer isn't going to hire you with God whispering in his ear? And who doesn't want God guiding the scalpel during surgery?

Now, this is not a quick, "God please help so and so during her interview." This is a group of people all praying at the same time, for the entire duration of the interview. Total devotion to lifting you up to God for a specific purpose. Next time you have a life event, ask friends and family to pray you through it. Just the knowledge that they are reaching out to God on your behalf, will make you stronger to face whatever the event may be.

"God, help me to be a Warrior for others. Help me to know what to say and how to proceed. I know you are listening to all your children and are there through every need. Help me to lift up all of your children in prayer. Amen."

Prayer Prompts:
Pray for God to teach you how to be a warrior.
Pray for friends and family through life events.
Pray fervently to cover loved ones in need.

Notes:

Use this page to write out your prayer...

WISDOM

Psalm 90:12 Teach us to number our days, that we may gain a heart of wisdom.

So, what is wisdom? According to Mr. Webster, (Webster's dictionary) Wisdom is the quality of having experience, knowledge, and good judgment; the quality of being wise.

Ephesians 5:15, So be careful how you live. Do not live like fools, but like those who are wise. God gives us that wisdom. He will guide our lives in the right direction, all we need do, is ask. *Proverbs 2:6, For the Lord gives wisdom; from His mouth come knowledge and understanding.* Our God is an awesome God. He will help us to make wise choices, and forgives us, even when we do not.

Whenever I think about wisdom, the serenity prayer comes to mind. Let's use that as our starting point.

"God grant me the serenity to accept the things I cannot change, courage to change the things I can, and wisdom to know the difference." Add your personal touches here…Amen."

Prayer prompts:

Ask God to help you be wise in your decisions. Pray to make the right choices in upcoming events in your life.

A new job opportunity

A new relationship, or a current one...

He will guide you in every step of your life if you ask Him. Make a list of the things going on in your life. Things that you can ask God to guide you through.

Notes:

Use this page to write out your prayer...

"WWJD"

If you are going to walk the walk, and talk the talk, make sure you're speaking God's language. Ask yourself, what would Jesus do? Well, if you have to ask, you probably shouldn't do it. *James 4:17, Anyone, then, who knows the good he ought to do and doesn't do it, sins.*

Jesus was sent to us as a baby, grew up in a humble home, then went off to preach to the people. This sinless man was sent here for one purpose, to die for all of our sins. *Luke 2:40, And the child grew and became strong; he was filled with wisdom, and the grace of God was upon him.*

Mark 10:45, For even the son of man did not come to be served, but to serve, and to give his life as a ransom for many. Jesus was a man, that simple. He didn't come to be praised or glorified. Even the miracles he performed, were not for his glory. They were to help others. To heal the sick, help the blind to see, and even feed a crowd. His actions were for our benefit not his own.

That is how God wants us to live. To be like Christ, to live a Christlike life. To show love and mercy to others. Help our neighbors, not criticize them. Feed the hungry and clothe the homeless. Volunteer at a shelter in your area. Serve others, not yourself.

"God, help me to be like Jesus. Show me how to serve others and show love and compassion to those around me. Amen."

Prayer Prompts:
Pray for the homeless in your area
Pray that God will show you ways to serve

Notes:

Use this page to write out your prayer...

X GAMES

If you've ever watched the X Games, you know it takes hard work and dedication to succeed. The contestants practice day and night for years to perfect their craft. *Romans 5:3-4, "Not only so, but also glory in our sufferings, because we know that suffering produces perseverance; perseverance, character; and character, hope.*

Tony Hawk didn't just pick up a skateboard one day and become an instant superstar. He worked hard for years to be able to compete at the X Games level. Travis Pastrana started riding a one-speed motorcycle at age 4. He grew up competing from an early age and has excelled at anything with gas and wheels. From motocross to NASCAR, he pushes everything beyond the limit. Travis didn't win 11 gold medals at X Games without a lot of hard work and broken bones, several actually. But he didn't give up, he still looks for tricks that no one else has tried.

Matthew 19:26, Jesus looked at them and said, "with man this is impossible, but with God all things are possible." God makes everything possible but that doesn't mean we don't have to work for it just that he will help us through it. It doesn't have to be extreme or life threatening for him to give us strength. God is with us through everything we do. *Philippians 4:13, "I can do all things through him who gives me strength."*

"Lord, I ask that you give me the courage of a champion. Strength that I might be able to step out of my comfort zone to share You with others. You are my rock and my salvation. I praise you for all the wonders you have created. Amen."

Prayer Prompts:
Everyone benefits from prayer. If you have a favorite athlete or even the whole team, add them to your prayer list.
Pray for people in India who risk their lives every day to worship Jesus.
Pray for your pastor and staff that God will give them strength and courage to go out and spread the news of Jesus.

Notes:

Use this page to write out your prayer...

X MARKS THE SPOT

Matthew 6:21, For where your treasure is, there your heart will be also.

Have you ever searched for buried treasure? Or at least watched a pirate movie? There is always an old worn out map, with the cliché X, to mark where the treasure lies. So, what is your treasure, your passion? If it happens to be a mission trip somewhere, put an X on the map. For most of us it will be a virtual X, but we can claim it just the same. Throughout our lives, we may be passionate about several things. There is one treasure we can all agree on. God is our treasure, therefore our heart is on God, so our X is on God.

Now follow the map...John 14:6, Jesus answered, "I am the way and the truth and the life. No one comes to the Father except through me." It's that simple. We follow Jesus and we have a home in Heaven with God.

"Lord, I lift up songs of praise in your Holy Name. Thank you for all you have done for me today. You are my way, my truth, and my life. I ask that you give me guidance and light my path, so that I may follow you through any storm. Amen"

Prayer Prompts: This one is personal
What are your dreams and passions?
Are you following the path God has laid out for you?
Does God come first in your life?

Notes:

Use this page to write out your prayer...

YAHTZEE

Proverbs 11:14, "without good direction, people lose their way; the more wise council you follow, the better your chances."

Yahtzee is a game of chance. You roll 5 dice and score points depending on the combination of numbers after three rolls. A Yahtzee is when all five dice are the same and is worth 50 points.

Luckily, getting into heaven doesn't rely on a toss of the dice. We don't have to take chances; we just have to believe. *Romans 10:9, "Because if you confess with your mouth that Jesus is Lord and believe in your heart that God raised him from the dead, you will be saved.*

Our sins have all been forgiven because Jesus died on the cross, but that is not the ultimate prize. *John 3:16, "For God so love the world, that He gave His only son, that whoever believes in Him should not perish but have eternal life."*

John 17:3, And this is eternal life, that they know you, the only true God and Jesus Christ, whom you have sent. Andrew Wommack explains eternal life as this. "When Jesus said eternal life was knowing God, he was Speaking of having an intimate, close, personal relationship with God. That's awesome!"

We are so precious to God that we can have a personal relationship with Him. There is no prize greater than that.

"Father in heaven, we are grateful to be your children. To be able to talk to you and listen for your response. To give you glory and honor and to praise your name. Thank you Jesus for giving us life eternal through your death, so that we can truly live in you. Amen."

Prayer Prompts:
List the names of friends and family who do not have that one-on-one bond with Christ. Pray for them to understand and accept that Jesus suffered for all mankind. That we are all God's children. And He loves us each the same.

Notes:

Use this page to write out your prayer...

YOU

Jeremiah 4:14, "O Jerusalem, wash the evil from your heart and be saved. How long will you Harbor wicked thoughts?"

Not we, us, or they, but you! Most of the time we talk about all Christians as a whole. It's time to look at each one as an individual child of God. Today it's about you! Your personal relationship with God.

Galatians 3:26, "For in Christ Jesus you are all sons of God, through faith." What does it mean to have a personal relationship with God? It means He loves you unconditionally, and that you love Him. We praise Him and worship Him, as well as ask for His wisdom and guidance through prayer. *Hebrews 13:5, "I will never leave you nor forsake you."* God will always watch out for you in return for your faithfulness. It is time to get on your knees, bow your head, and thank God for all the little things He has done for you. Praise His name!

"Lord, I thank you for this beautiful day. The sunshine, the gentle rain, together bring a sense of peace. I love you Lord; your mercy and grace carry me through the rough times. You are always with me, guiding me, nudging me toward the path you have chosen just for me. Amen."

Prayer Prompts:
Make it personal. Pray for yourself and immediate family.
Thank God for your family, and for all He has given you.
Pray for wisdom and guidance. (we can never get enough of that)
Pray for ways to help others.

Notes:

Use this page to write out your prayer...

ZACCHAEUS

In Luke 19, Jesus is passing through Jericho. As always, He is surrounded by a crowd. Zacchaeus, the tax collector, and reportedly a small man, climbed a tree so he could see Jesus through the masses.

Luke 19:5-7, When Jesus reached the spot, he looked up and said to him, "Zacchaeus, come down immediately. I must stay at your house today." So, he came down at once and welcomed him gladly. All the people saw this and began to mutter, "He has gone to be the guest of a sinner".

Zacchaeus climbed down and stood before the Lord. He immediately repented, offering to repay four times the amount to anyone he cheated and to give half his possessions to the poor.

Luke 19:9-10, Jesus said to him, "Today salvation has come to this house, because this man, too, is a son of Abraham. For the Son of Man came to seek and to save what was lost."

Jesus was not sent here to preach to the prophets and the holy men. He was sent to redeem the sinners through His blood on the cross. *Romans 3:23, For all have sinned, and come short of the Glory of God.*

"Lord, we are all sinners like Zacchaeus. We ask you to open our hearts to Jesus, and we thank you for sending Him to free us from sin and death. Amen."

Prayer Prompts:
Pray for forgiveness, and for strength to forgive those who have wronged you.
Pray for courage to ask forgiveness of those you have done wrong to.
Give God PRAISE! Thank Him for sending Jesus.

Notes:

Use this page to write out your prayer...

ZEAL

Zeal, great energy, or enthusiasm in pursuit of a cause or objective, passion.

What do you have a passion for? Do you have a zeal, or passion, for your job? How about your hobbies? Sports, camping, hunting, fishing? Sewing, painting, puzzles? For me, it's any kind of craft. I like to sew, paint, and scrapbook, unfortunately I haven't found a way to turn my passions into a paying job, so for now they're hobbies.

My main passion is sharing Jesus. I have a zeal for telling others what amazing things God can do in their lives. Our zeal, or passion for Christ is what makes us Christians. We love our Lord and He loves us.

Romans 10:2, "For I bear them witness that they have a zeal for God, but not according to knowledge."

Our enthusiasm to share Christ is contagious. We teach someone about Jesus, and they in turn want to share with others. There is no greater feeling than bringing a new lamb into the fold. Seeing their excitement as they learn what God has done for them so that they can have a life in heaven. That their sins are all forgiven, and they get to begin again baptized in the Holy Spirit.

"Father, thank you for your sacrifices. Because of your son, we all have the opportunity for eternal life. And Lord, while I am on this earth, I asked for courage and faith to step out of my comfort zone and share your love with others. Amen."

Prayer Prompts:
Pray for a zeal to share Christ
Pray for a passion to read God's word daily
Pray for the opportunity to spread your enthusiasm of God's love

Notes:

Use this page to write out your prayer...

ZION

Psalm 48:2, Beautiful in elevation, is the joy of all the earth, Mount Zion, in the far north, the city of the great King. Zion in the Old Testament is the easternmost of the two hills of ancient Jerusalem. It is the name of the hill upon which Jerusalem was built.

Isaiah 28:16, Therefore thus says the Lord God, "Behold, I am the one who has laid as a foundation in Zion, a stone, a tested stone, a precious cornerstone, of a pure foundation; Whoever believes will not be in haste." With Jesus as our cornerstone, we too, are on firm foundation

We can feel secure in the knowledge that our God loves and protects us. Zion isn't just a place, it's also the people. We all have wonderful people in our lives. If we surround ourselves with good Christian friends, we will feel encouraged and up-lifted. Live as an example to others and let them see Jesus in your everyday life. Let the radiance of Zion reflect in you!

"Holy Lord, thank you for providing us a firm foundation on which to thrive. We feel secure in the knowledge that you will provide and protect as we go forth into this world to proclaim your grace. Let your light shine in us as a beacon to those who still need to know you. Amen."

Prayer Prompts:
Courage to step out of the comfort zone and tell others how great our God is.
Faith to know God will be there in all we do.
Grace to forgive those who wrong us
Humility to ask forgiveness of those we've wronged.
Wisdom to know when to speak and when to listen.

Notes:

Use this page to write out your prayer...